The Fit and Healthy Slow Cooker Cookbook

Super Tasty Homemade Recipes To Save Time and Lose Weight

Laurel Twitty

rendering of legal, financial, medical or professional advice. The content within this book has been derived from various sources. Please consult a licensed professional before attempting any techniques outlined in this book.

By reading this document, the reader agrees that under no circumstances is the author responsible for any losses, direct or indirect, which are incurred as a result of the use of information contained within this document, including, but not limited to, — errors, omissions, or inaccuracies.

Table of contents

Chicken Curry

Preparation time: 15 minutes

Cooking time: 6 hours

Servings: 4 people

Ingredients:

- 2 pounds of chicken breasts/thighs
- 2 cups full fat coconut milk
- 6 cups, your choice, fresh vegetables
- 1 tablespoon cumin
- 1 cup tomato sauce
- 2 teaspoons ground ginger
- 2 teaspoons ground coriander
- 1 teaspoon cinnamon
- 2 teaspoons garlic powder
- 1 cup of water
- ½ teaspoon cayenne pepper
- pinch of salt and fresh ground pepper, each

Directions:

1. Rinse the chicken, pat dry. Dice the vegetables and chicken into chunks. Place all the fixings in your slow cooker.
2. Add the coconut milk, tomatoes, and spices. Add the cup of water. Cover and cook on low within 6 hours. Serve hot—side with rice or greens.

Nutrition: Calories 515 Fat 29.3g Carb 23.2g Protein 39.8g

Stuffed Chicken Breasts

Preparation time: 15 minutes

Cooking time: 6 hours

Servings: 2-4 people

Ingredients:

- 6 boneless chicken breasts
- 1/3 cup feta cheese, crumbled
- 1-2 teaspoons fresh oregano
- pinch of salt, fresh ground pepper, each
- 1 tablespoon olive oil
- ½ onion, diced
- 2 teaspoons minced garlic
- ¾ cup fresh spinach
- juice of 1 lemon
- 2 pepperoncini peppers
- ½ red pepper, diced
- 1 cup chicken stock
- ½ cup white wine

Directions:

1. Rinse the chicken, pat dry. Slice the chicken breasts ¾ open. Leave them attached. In a large bowl, combine feta cheese, oregano, salt, and pepper.

2. In a large skillet, heat the olive oil. Add the onion, cook 2 minutes, then put the garlic, cook 1 minute. Add the spinach. Heat until the spinach wilts.

3. Add the spinach batter to the bowl with feta cheese. Add the lemon juice, pepperoncini peppers, red pepper. Stir to combine.
4. Stuff the chicken breasts with the mixture. Place them in the slow cooker. Pour in chicken stock and wine—cover and cook on for 6 hours, then serve hot—side with salad.

Nutrition: Calories 357 Fat 15.2g Carbohydrates 5.2g Protein 44.8g

Chicken Hearts

Preparation time: 15 minutes

Cooking time: 8 hours

Servings: 2 people

Ingredients:

- 2 pounds of chicken hearts
- 1 onion, sliced
- 1-pound mushrooms, sliced
- 4 garlic cloves, minced
- 1 tablespoon Dijon mustard
- 1 teaspoon salt, fresh ground pepper, each
- ½ tablespoon paprika
- ½ tablespoon cayenne pepper
- 1 cup chicken stock
- ¼ cup of coconut milk
- 7 ounces' Greek yogurt, full fat

Directions:

1. Rinse the chicken, pat dry. Place all the ingredients, up to the chicken stock, in a slow cooker. Cover and cook on low within 8 hours.
2. Once finished cooking, stir in the cream and yogurt, wait 10 minutes and serve—side with potatoes, greens.

Nutrition: Calories 241 Fat 11.8g Carbohydrates 20.4g Protein 14.8g

Honey Chicken Drumsticks

Preparation time: 15 minutes

Cooking time: 6 hours

Servings: 2-4 people

Ingredients:

- 8 chicken drumsticks
- 1 tablespoon honey
- 3 apples, peeled and diced
- ½ teaspoon cinnamon
- 1 teaspoon salt
- Garnish: chopped parsley, sesame seeds

Directions:

1. Rinse the chicken, pat dry. Mix the honey and salt in a medium bowl. Pour mixture over the drumsticks.
2. Place the drumsticks in the slow cooker. Cover and cook on low within 6 hours, until chicken is tender. Serve hot. Garnish with parsley and sesame seeds.

Nutrition: Calories 259 Fat 5.6g Carbohydrates 27.7g Protein 25.8g

Rosemary Lemon Chicken

Preparation time: 15 minutes

Cooking time: 6 hours

Servings: 4 people

Ingredients:

- 4 pounds of chicken thighs, bone & skin in
- 1 tablespoon olive oil
- Pinch of sea salt and ground black pepper, each
- ½ cup of preferred flour
- 3 medium yellow onions, sliced
- 8 carrots, sliced
- 6 garlic cloves, chopped
- 3 springs rosemary
- ½ cup lime juice
- ¾ cup chicken broth
- 1 tablespoon lemon zest
- 1 lemon sliced

Directions:

1. Rinse the chicken, pat dry. Place the chicken, salt, pepper, onions, carrots in your slow cooker. Sprinkle the flour over ingredients. Stir until they are coated.

2. Add garlic, rosemary, lime juice, broth, lemon zest, sliced lemon. Cover and cook on low within 6 hours, until chicken is tender. Serve hot.

Nutrition: Calories 510 Fat 14g Carbohydrates 24.7g Protein 63g

Salsa Chicken

Preparation time: 15 minutes

Cooking time: 6 hours

Servings: 4 people

Ingredients:

- 4 chicken thighs
- salad greens
- 1 pint of salsa
- shredded cheese

Directions:

1. Rinse the chicken, pat dry. Place the chicken, greens, and salsa in the slow cooker. Cook on low for 6 hours. Garnish with cheese.

Nutrition: Calories 310 Fat 10.9g Carbohydrates 7.1g Protein 44.6g

Turmeric Chicken

Preparation time: 15 minutes

Cooking time: 5 hours

Servings: 4 people

Ingredients:

- 5 pounds of chicken, organic
- 1 teaspoon turmeric
- ½ cup coconut milk, full fat
- 4 garlic cloves, finely grated
- 2-3-inch fresh ginger, grated
- Pinch of salt and fresh ground pepper, each
- Garnish: Scallions

Directions:

1. In the slow cooker, combine the turmeric, ginger, and garlic. Stir in the coconut milk. Season chicken with salt and pepper. Place in the slow cooker. Cook on low within 5 hours, until chicken cooked. Shred with 2 forks.

Nutrition: Calories 359 Fat 7.7g Carbohydrates 2.1g Protein 66g

Marinara Chicken

Preparation time: 15 minutes

Cooking time: 4 hours

Servings: 4 people

Ingredients:

- 4 pounds of chicken
- 1 jar marinara sauce
- 1 onion, diced
- 2 garlic cloves, diced
- ½ green pepper, diced
- 2 zucchinis, diced
- ¼ cup basil
- Pinch of salt and fresh ground pepper, each
- Garnish: Parmigiano Reggiano, grated

Directions:

1. Rinse the chicken, pat dry. Season the chicken with salt and pepper. Place in the slow cooker. Add the onions, garlic, green pepper, and zucchini.
2. Pour the marinara sauce over the ingredients. Cover and cook on medium within 4 hours, until cooked through.
3. Shred the chicken with 2 forks. Serve warm over favorite pasta. Top with Parmigiano Reggiano.

Nutrition: Calories 319 Fat 6.1g Carbohydrates 8.9g Protein 54.5g

Chocolate Chicken

Preparation time: 15 minutes

Cooking time: 6 hours

Servings: 2-4 people

Ingredients:

- 2 pounds' chicken breasts, bone-in
- Pinch of sea salt, fresh ground pepper, each
- 2 tablespoons ghee
- 1 medium onion, diced
- 4 garlic cloves, minced
- 7 medium tomatoes, peeled and chopped
- 2 1/2 ounces of dark chocolate, crumbled
- 5 dried chili peppers, finely chopped
- 1 teaspoon cumin powder
- ¼ cup Almond Butter
- ½ teaspoon cinnamon powder
- 1/2 teaspoon guajillo chili powder
- Garnish: diced Avocado, chopped cilantro, and diced jalapeno pepper, seeds out

Directions:

1. Rinse the chicken, pat dry. Place all the other fixings in the slow cooker. Cover and cook on low within 6 hours. Serve warm. Garnish with avocado chunks, cilantro, and diced jalapeno.

Nutrition: Calories 477 Fat 20.6g Carbohydrates 19.6g Protein 53.4g

Coconut Curried Chicken

Preparation time: 15 minutes

Cooking time: 5 hours

Servings: 4 people

Ingredients:

- 3 pounds of chicken breasts/thighs
- 1 large onion, chopped
- 2 small carrots, chopped
- 2 garlic cloves, minced
- 1 tablespoon curry powder
- 1 tablespoon mustard condiment
- ½ cup coconut cream
- ½ cup chicken stock
- 2 tablespoons ghee
- Pinch of salt
- 2 Yukon gold potatoes, peeled, chopped
- Garnish: chopped parsley

Directions:

1. Rinse the chicken, pat dry. Place all the fixings, except the potatoes, in the slow cooker. Stir well. After 3 hours of cooking, add the potatoes. Cover and cook on low within 4-5 hours, until chicken and potatoes are tender. Serve warm.

Nutrition: Calories 377 Fat 25g Carbohydrates 6.3g Protein 30.4g

Buffalo Chicken

Preparation time: 15 minutes

Cooking time: 6 hours

Servings: 2-4 people

Ingredients:

- ½ pound chicken breast, boneless, skinless
- ½ pound chicken thighs, boneless, skinless
- 1/3 cup hot sauce
- 1 tablespoon coconut aminos
- 2 tablespoons ghee
- ¼ teaspoon cayenne
- ½ teaspoon garlic powder
- 4 small sweet potatoes, chopped
- ¼ - ½ cup of water
- Garnish: ranch dressing, chives

Directions:

1. Rinse the chicken, pat dry. In a skillet, combine the ghee, garlic powder, hot sauce, cayenne, and coconut aminos. Simmer for 5 minutes.
2. Coat the chicken with the mixture—place in the slow cooker. Add the potatoes, then pour in ¼ cup of water.
3. Cover and cook on low within 5-6 hours, until chicken cooked. Serve warm. Garnish with ranch dressing, chives.

Nutrition: Calories 423 Fat 11.4g Carbohydrates 56.4g Protein 24.1g

Teriyaki Chicken

Preparation time: 15 minutes

Cooking time: 6 hours

Servings: 4 people

Ingredients:

- 2 pounds' chicken thighs, boneless, skinless
- 3 tablespoons honey
- ½ cup coconut aminos
- 1 ½ teaspoons minced ginger
- 4 garlic cloves, minced
- 1 tablespoon sesame seeds, toasted
- 1 teaspoon of sea salt

Directions:

1. Rinse the chicken, pat dry. Place all the fixings, except sesame seeds, in the slow cooker. Cook on low within 5-6 hours, until chicken cooked through.
2. Cut the chicken into bite-size pieces. Garnish with sesame seeds. Serve warm on a bed of rice.

Nutrition: Calories 341 Fat 12g Carbohydrates 11.7g Protein 44.2g

Pulled BBQ Chicken

Preparation time: 15 minutes

Cooking time: 4 hours

Servings: 2-4 people

Ingredients:

- 3 pounds of chicken breasts
- 2 cups tomatoes, diced
- 3-4 pitted dates
- 3 garlic cloves, minced
- ½ large yellow onion, diced
- 3 tablespoons apple cider vinegar
- 2 teaspoons sea salt
- 1 tablespoon smoked paprika
- 6 ounces' tomato paste
- 1 ½ tablespoon avocado oil

Directions:

1. Rinse the chicken, pat dry. Drizzle the chicken with avocado oil. Place in the slow cooker. Blend the rest of the ingredients in a food processor. Pour over chicken. Cook on low for 4 hours. Shred with 2 forks. Serve hot.

Nutrition: Calories 217 Fat 6.3g Carbohydrates 19.6g Protein 22.1g

Lemon Thyme Chicken

Preparation time: 15 minutes

Cooking time: 4 hours

Servings: 4 people

Ingredients:

- 4-pound chicken
- ¼ cup lemon juice
- 1 teaspoon dried thyme
- 2-3 bay leaves
- 5 garlic cloves, diced
- 1 teaspoon of sea salt
- ¼ teaspoon black pepper
- ¼ cup of water

Directions:

1. Rinse the chicken, pat dry. Place in the slow cooker. Pour lemon juice over the chicken. Season with thyme, salt, and pepper. Add bay leaves, garlic.
2. Put the water in the bottom of the slow cooker. Cover and cook for 4 hours, until chicken is cooked through. Serve hot.

Nutrition: Calories 276 Fat 5.6g Carbohydrates 0.3g Protein 52.7g

Sweet & Smoky Pulled Chicken

Preparation time: 5 minutes

Cooking time: 7 hours & 5 minutes

Servings: 4 people

Ingredients:

- 1-pound pasture-raised chicken breasts, skinless
- 13 1/2 fluid ounce tomato passata, unsweetened
- 1 teaspoon garlic powder
- 1 teaspoon of sea salt
- 1 teaspoon ground black pepper
- ½ cup apple cider vinegar
- 3 tablespoon Swerve sweeteners
- 1/4 tsp cayenne pepper
- 1 tablespoon smoked paprika
- 3 tablespoons coconut aminos
- ½ cup avocado oil
- 1 cup sour cream for serving

Directions:

1. Put the chicken breast in your slow cooker. Whisk together remaining ingredients except for sour cream and pour over chicken.
2. Shut with lid and cook for 6 to 7 hours at low heat setting or 2 to 4 hours at high heat setting or until cooked. When done, transfer chicken to a cutting board and shred with two forks.

26

3. Transfer sauce in the slow cooker to a saucepan and simmer for 3 minutes or more.

4. Spoon this sauce over chicken, stir until chicken is coated with sauce. Add a little more oil, toss until combined, then top with sour cream and serve straightaway.

Nutrition: Calories: 234 Fat: 12g Protein: 27.5g Carbs: 4g

Mexican Chicken Fajita Soup

Preparation time: 5 minutes

Cooking time: 6 hours

Servings: 4 people

Slow cooker size : 6-quart

Ingredients:

- 2 pasture-raised chicken breasts, skinless
- 2 tablespoons cashew butter
- 1 medium red bell pepper, diced
- 1/2 small white onion, diced
- 1 teaspoon minced garlic
- 10-ounce tomatoes & chilies
- 1 tablespoon taco seasoning
- 1 cup chicken broth
- 2/3 cup and 1 tablespoon cream cheese
- 1/2 cup heavy whipping cream
- 4 tablespoons sour cream for topping

Directions:

1. Put a large skillet pan on medium heat, add butter and when it melts, add pepper, onion, garlic, taco seasoning and cook for 3 minutes or until fragrant and onion are slightly tender.

2. Spoon this mixture in a 6-quart slow cooker, add chicken, tomato, chilies, and broth, and shut with

28

lid. Plugin the slow cooker and cook chicken for 4 to 6 hours at a low heat setting or until chicken is tender.

3. When done, stir in cream cheese and heavy cream until creamy, then top with sour cream and serve.

Nutrition: Calories: 476 Fat: 35.9g Protein: 31.8g Carbs: 10.8g

Creamy Tuscan Garlic Chicken

Preparation time: 15 minutes

Cooking time: 8 hours & 10 minutes

Servings: 4 people

Slow cooker size: 6-quart

Ingredients:

- 4 large pasture-raised chicken breast, each about 6 ounces
- 1/2 cup sun-dried tomatoes, chopped
- 2 cup spinach, chopped
- 3 teaspoons minced garlic
- 1 ½ teaspoon sea salt
- 1 teaspoon ground black pepper
- 1 tablespoon Italian seasoning
- 1 tablespoon avocado oil
- 1 cup heavy cream
- 1/3 cup chicken broth
- 3/4 cup grated parmesan cheese

Directions:

1. Put oil in your saucepan on medium heat, then put garlic and cook for 1 minute or until fragrant.
2. Whisk in cream and broth, bring the mixture to simmer, reduce heat to a low level, and simmer more for 10 minutes or until sauce thickens enough to coat the spoon's back.

3. place the chicken in a 6-quarts slow cooker. When the sauce is ready, stir in cheese until smooth, and then pour it over the chicken.
4. Cook within 6 to 8 hours at low heat setting or 3 to 4 hours at high heat setting or until cooked. When done, transfer chicken to a serving plate and set aside.
5. Add spinach to the sauce in the slow cooker and cook for 3 to 5 minutes or until spinach leaves wilt. Spoon sauce over chicken, then top with tomatoes and serve.

Nutrition: Calories: 531 Fat: 35g Protein: 45g Carbs: 9g

Chicken Stew

Preparation time: 5 minutes

Cooking time: 2 hours & 10 minutes

Servings: 4 people

Slow cooker size: 6-quart

Ingredients:

- 28 ounces' skinless pasture-raised chicken thighs, diced into 1-inch pieces
- ½ cup chopped white onion
- 1 cup fresh spinach
- 2 sticks of celery, diced
- 1 ½ teaspoon minced garlic
- 1 teaspoon salt
- ½ teaspoon ground black pepper
- ½ teaspoon dried rosemary
- ¼ teaspoon dried thyme
- ½ teaspoon dried oregano
- 2 cups chicken stock
- ½ cup heavy cream

Directions:

1. Place all the ingredients except for spinach and cream in a 6-quart slow cooker and shut with a lid. Cook for 4 hours at a low heat setting or 2 hours at a high heat setting or until cooked.

2. Then stir in spinach and cream and cook for 5 to 10 minutes at a high heat setting or until spinach leaves wilt. Serve straight away.

Nutrition: Calories: 356 Fat: 24g Protein: 31g Carbs: 6g

Curried Chicken Tacos

Preparation time: 5 minutes

Cooking time: 8 hours

Servings: 4 people

Slow cooker size: 6-quart

Ingredients:

- For Curried Chicken:
- 2 pounds' skinless pasture-raised chicken breasts
- 15-ounce diced tomatoes
- 3 chilis de Arbor, chopped
- 1/2 of medium white onion, chopped
- 2 teaspoon grated ginger
- 2 teaspoons minced garlic
- 1 teaspoon salt
- 1 1/2 teaspoons ground turmeric
- 2 teaspoons ground cumin
- 1 tablespoon ground coriander
- 1/4 teaspoon cinnamon
- 1/4 teaspoon ground cardamom
- 2-star anise
- 1/2 cup chicken stock
- For Avocado Cream:
- 1 large avocado, pitted
- 1/3 cup chopped cilantro
- 2 teaspoons onion powder

- 1/2 teaspoon salt
- 1 1/2 teaspoons red chili powder
- 5 tablespoons yogurt, high-fat
- 1 1/2 tablespoons lemon juice
- For Taco:
- 1/2 of small red cabbage, sliced
- 8 large leaves of collard greens
- 1 large red pepper, sliced
- 2 cups sour cream

Directions:

1. Place all the ingredients, except for star anise, and stock in a 6-quart slow cooker and toss until just mixed. Then pour in chicken stock, add star anise, and shut with lid.
2. Cook within 7 to 8 hours at low heat setting or 4 to5 hours at high heat setting.
3. For the avocado cream, place the ingredients for avocado cream in a food processor and pulse for 1 to 2 minutes or until smooth; set aside until required.
4. Trim the tough stem from collard greens, rinse well, pat dry, and set aside until required. When chicken is cooked, shred with two forks and toss until coated with sauce.
5. Arrange collard greens in a clean working space, then top with chicken, cabbage, pepper, avocado

cream, and sour cream in the end. Serve straight away.

Nutrition: Calories: 371.25 Fat: 19g Protein: 41g Carbs: 9g

Mushrooms Snapper

Preparation time: 15 minutes

Cooking time: 6 hours

Servings: 4 people

Ingredients:

- 1 cup sour cream
- 1 onion, diced
- ¼ cup almond milk
- 1 tsp salt
- 7 oz cremini mushrooms
- 1 tsp ground thyme
- 1 tbsp ground paprika
- 1 tsp ground coriander
- 1 tsp kosher salt
- 1 tbsp lemon juice
- 1 tsp butter
- 1 lb. snapper, chopped
- 1 tsp lemon zest

Directions:

1. Season the snapper with thyme, paprika, coriander, salt, lemon zest, and lemon juice in a bowl. Cover the snapper and marinate it for 10 minutes.
2. Grease the insert of the slow cooker with butter and add a snapper mixture. Add cremini mushrooms, onion, almond milk, and sour cream.

3. Put the cooker's lid on and set the cooking time to 6 hours on low. Serve warm.

Nutrition: Calories: 248 Fat: 6.3g Carbs: 31.19g Protein: 20g

Orange Cod

Preparation time: 15 minutes

Cooking time: 3 hours

Servings: 4 people

Ingredients:

- 1-pound cod fillet, chopped
- 2 oranges, chopped
- 1 tablespoon maple syrup
- 1 cup of water
- 1 garlic clove, diced
- 1 teaspoon ground black pepper

Directions:

1. Mix cod with ground black pepper and transfer to the slow cooker. Add garlic, water, maple syrup, and oranges. Close the lid and cook the meal on high for 3 hours.

Nutrition: Calories 150 Protein 21.2g Carbohydrates 14.8g Fat 1.2g

Cod with Shrimp Sauce

Preparation time: 15 minutes

Cooking time : 2 hours

Servings: 4 people

Ingredients:

- 1 lb. cod fillets, cut into medium pieces
- 2 tbsp parsley, chopped
- 4 oz. breadcrumbs
- 2 tsp lemon juice
- 2 eggs, whisked
- 2 oz. butter, melted
- ½ pint milk
- ½ pint shrimp sauce
- Salt and black pepper to the taste

Directions:

1. Toss fish with crumbs, parsley, salt, black pepper, and lemon juice in a suitable bowl. Add butter, milk, egg, and fish mixture to the insert of the slow cooker.
2. Put the cooker's lid on and set the cooking time to 2 hours on high. Serve warm.

Nutrition: Calories: 231 Fat: 3g Carbs: 10g Protein: 5g

Baked Cod

Preparation time: 15 minutes

Cooking time: 5 hours

Servings: 2 people

Ingredients:

- 2 cod fillets
- 2 teaspoons cream cheese
- 2 tablespoons bread crumbs
- 1 teaspoon salt
- ½ teaspoon cayenne pepper
- 2 oz Mozzarella, shredded

Directions:

1. Sprinkle the cod fillets with cayenne pepper and salt. Put the fish in the slow cooker. Then top it with cream cheese, bread crumbs, and mozzarella. Close the lid and cook the meal for 5 hours on low. Serve.

Nutrition: Calories 210 Protein 29.2g Carbohydrates 6.2g Fat 7.6g

Cod Sticks

Preparation time : 15 minutes

Cooking time: 1 hour & 30 minutes

Servings: 2 people

Ingredients:

- 2 cod fillets
- 1 teaspoon ground black pepper
- 1 egg, beaten
- 1/3 cup breadcrumbs
- 1 tablespoon coconut oil
- ¼ cup of water

Directions:

1. Cut the cod fillets into medium sticks and sprinkle with ground black pepper. Dip or soak the fish in the beaten egg, then coat in the breadcrumbs.
2. Pour water into the slow cooker. Add coconut oil and fish sticks. Cook the meal on high for 1 hour and 30 minutes. Serve.

Nutrition: Calories 254 Protein 25.3g Carbohydrates 13.8g Fat 11g

Hot Salmon and Carrots

Preparation time: 15 minutes

Cooking time: 3 hours

Servings: 2 people

Ingredients:

- 1-pound salmon fillets, boneless
- 1 cup baby carrots, peeled
- ½ teaspoon hot paprika
- ½ teaspoon chili powder
- ¼ cup chicken stock
- 2 scallions, chopped
- 1 tablespoon smoked paprika
- A pinch of salt and black pepper
- 2 tablespoons chives, chopped

Directions:

1. In your slow cooker, mix the salmon with the carrots, paprika, and the other ingredients, toss, put the lid on and cook on low for 3 hours. Divide the mix between plates and serve.

Nutrition: Calories 193 Fat 7g Carbs 6g Protein 6g

Chili-Rubbed Tilapia

Preparation time: 15 minutes

Cooking time: 4 hours

Servings: 4 people

Ingredients:

- 2 tablespoons chili powder
- ½ teaspoon garlic powder
- 1-pound tilapia
- 2 tablespoons lemon juice
- 2 tablespoons olive oil

Directions:

1. Place all ingredients in a mixing bowl. Stir to combine everything. Marinate in the fridge within 15 minutes.
2. Get a foil and place the fish, including the marinade, in the middle of the foil. Fold the foil and crimp the edges to seal. Place inside the slow cooker—cook on high for 2 hours or on low for 4 hours.

Nutrition: Calories: 183 Carbohydrates: 2.9g Protein: 23.4g Fat: 11.3g

Fish Mix

Preparation time: 15 minutes

Cooking time: 2 hours & 30 minutes

Servings: 4 people

Ingredients:

- 4 white fish fillets, skinless and boneless
- ½ teaspoon mustard seeds
- Salt and black pepper to the taste
- 2 green chilies, chopped
- 1 teaspoon ginger, grated
- 1 teaspoon curry powder
- ¼ teaspoon cumin, ground
- 2 tablespoons olive oil
- 1 small red onion, chopped
- 1-inch turmeric root, grated
- ¼ cup cilantro, chopped
- 1 and ½ cups of coconut cream
- 3 garlic cloves, minced

Directions:

1. Heat a slow cooker with half of the oil over medium heat, add mustard seeds, ginger, onion, garlic, turmeric, chilies, curry powder, and cumin, stir and cook for 3-4 minutes.
2. Add the rest of the oil to your slow cooker, add spice mix, fish, coconut milk, salt, pepper, cover, and

cook on High for 2 hours and 30 minutes. Divide into bowls and serve with the cilantro sprinkled on top.

Nutrition: Calories 500 Fat 34g Carbs 13g Protein 44g

Chili Bigeye Jack (Tuna)

Preparation time: 15 minutes

Cooking time: 3 hours & 30 minutes

Servings: 4 people

Ingredients:

- 9 oz tuna fillet (bigeye jack), roughly chopped
- 1 teaspoon chili powder
- 1 teaspoon curry paste
- ½ cup of coconut milk
- 1 tablespoon sesame oil

Directions:

1. Mix curry paste plus coconut milk and pour the liquid into the slow cooker. Add tuna fillet and sesame oil. Then add chili powder. Cook the meal on high for 3 hours and 30 minutes. Serve.

Nutrition: Calories 341 Protein 14.2g Carbohydrates 2.4g Fat 31.2g

Smoked Trout

Preparation time : 3 minutes

Cooking time: 2 hours

Servings: 4

Ingredients:

- 2 tablespoons of liquid smoke
- 2 tablespoons olive oil
- 4 ounces smoked trout; skin removed then flaked
- Salt and pepper to taste
- 2 tablespoons mustard

Directions:

1. Place all ingredients in the slow cooker. Cook on high within 1 hour or low for 2 hours until the trout flakes have absorbed the sauce.

Nutrition: Calories: 116 Carbohydrates: 1.5g Protein: 7.2g Fat: 9.2g

Salmon with Green Peppercorn Sauce

Preparation time: 5 minutes

Cooking time: 3 hours

Servings: 4 people

Ingredients:

- 1 ¼ pounds salmon fillets, skin removed and cut into 4 portions
- Salt and pepper to taste
- 4 teaspoons unsalted butter
- ¼ cup lemon juice
- 1 teaspoon green peppercorns in vinegar

Directions:

1. Flavor the salmon fillets with salt plus pepper to taste. In a skillet, heat the butter and sear the salmon fillets for 2 minutes on each side.
2. Transfer in the slow cooker and pour the lemon juice and green peppercorns. Adjust the seasoning by adding in more salt or pepper depending on your taste. Cook on high within 1 hour or low for 3 hours.

Nutrition: Calories: 255 Carbohydrates: 2.3g Protein: 37.4g Fat: 13.5g

Coconut Curry Cod

Preparation time: 3 minutes

Cooking time: 4 hours

Servings: 4 people

Ingredients:

- 4 pieces of cod fillets
- Salt and pepper to taste
- 1 ½ cups coconut milk
- 2 teaspoons curry paste
- 2 teaspoons grated ginger

Directions

1. Place all ingredients in the slow cooker. Give a good stir. Cook on high within 2 hours or on low for 4 hours. Garnish with chopped cilantro if desired.

Nutrition: Calories: 296 Carbohydrates: 6.7g Protein: 20.1g Fat: 22.8g

Almond Crusted Tilapia

Preparation time: 5 minutes

Cooking time: 4 hours

Servings: 4 people

Ingredients:

- 2 tablespoons olive oil
- 1 cup chopped almonds
- ¼ cup ground flaxseed
- 4 tilapia fillets
- Salt and pepper to taste

Directions:

1. Arrange the bottom of the slow cooker with a foil. Grease the foil with olive oil. In a mixing bowl, combine the almonds and flaxseed.
2. Season the tilapia with salt and pepper to taste. Dredge the tilapia fillets with the almond and flaxseed mixture.
3. Place neatly in the foil-lined slow cooker—cook on high within 2 hours and low for 4 hours.

Nutrition: Calories: 233 Carbohydrates: 4.6g Protein: 25.5g Fat: 13.3g

Buttered Bacon and Scallops

Preparation time: 5 minutes

Cooking time: 2 hours

Servings: 4 people

Ingredients:

- 1 tablespoon butter
- 2 cloves of garlic, chopped
- 24 scallops, rinsed and patted dry
- Salt and pepper to taste
- 1 cup bacon, chopped

Directions:

1. In a skillet, heat the butter and sauté the garlic until fragrant and lightly browned. Transfer to a slow cooker and add the scallops.
2. Season with salt and pepper to taste. Cook on high within 45 minutes or low for 2 hours.
3. Meanwhile, cook the bacon until the fat has rendered and crispy. Sprinkle the cooked scallops with crispy bacon.

Nutrition: Calories: 261 Carbohydrates: 4.9 g Protein: 24.7 g Fat: 14.3 g

Lemony Shrimps in Hoisin Sauce

Preparation time: 3 minutes

Cooking time: 2 hours

Servings: 4 people

Ingredients:

- 1/3 cup hoisin sauce
- ½ cup lemon juice, freshly squeezed
- 1 ½ pounds shrimps, shelled and deveined
- Salt and pepper to taste
- 2 tablespoon cilantro leaves, chopped

Directions:

1. Into the slow cooker, place the hoisin sauce, lemon juice, and shrimps. Season with salt and pepper to taste.

2. Mix to incorporate all ingredients. Cook on high within 30 minutes or on low for 2 hours. Garnish with cilantro leaves.

Nutrition: Calories: 228 Carbohydrates: 6.3g Protein: 35.8g Fat: 3.2g

Creamy Seafood Chowder

Preparation time: 10 minutes

Cooking time: 5 hours

Servings: 6

Ingredients:

- Garlic – 5 cloves, crushed
- Small onion – 1, finely chopped
- Prawns – 1 cup
- Shrimp – 1 cup
- Whitefish – 1 cup
- Full-fat cream – 2 cups
- Dry white wine – 1 cup
- A handful of fresh parsley, finely chopped
- Olive oil – 2 tbsp.

Directions:

1. Drizzle oil into the Crock-Pot.
2. Add the white fish, shrimp, prawns, onion, garlic, cream, wine, salt, and pepper into the pot. Stir to mix.
3. Cover with the lid and cook on low for 5 hours.
4. Sprinkle with fresh parsley and serve.

Nutrition: Calories: 225 Fat: 9.6g Carbs: 5.6g Protein: 21.4g

Salmon Cake

Preparation time: 10 minutes

Cooking time: 4 hours

Servings: 4

Ingredients:

- Eggs – 4, lightly beaten
- Heavy cream – 3 tbsp.
- Baby spinach – 1 cup, roughly chopped
- Smoked salmon strips – 4 ounces, chopped
- A handful of fresh coriander, roughly chopped
- Olive oil – 2 tbsp.
- Salt and pepper to taste

Directions:

1. Drizzle oil into the Crock-Pot.
2. Place the spinach, cream, beaten egg, salmon, salt, and pepper into the pot and mix to combine.
3. Cover with the lid and cook on low for 4 hours.

Nutrition: Calories: 277 Fat: 20.8g Carbs: 1.1g Protein: 22.5g

Lemon-Butter Fish

Preparation time: 10 minutes

Cooking time: 5 hours

Servings: 4

Ingredients:

- Fresh white fish – 4 fillets
- Butter - 1 ½ ounce, soft but not melted
- Garlic cloves – 2, crushed
- Lemon – 1 (juice and zest)
- A handful of fresh parsley, finely chopped
- Salt and pepper to taste
- Olive oil – 2 tbsp.

Directions:

1. Combine the butter, garlic, zest of one lemon, and chopped parsley to a bowl.
2. Drizzle oil into the Crock-Pot.
3. Season the fish with salt and pepper and place into the pot.
4. Place a dollop of lemon butter onto each fish fillet and gently spread it out.
5. Cover with the lid and cook on low for 5 hours.
6. Serve each fish fillet with a generous spoonful of melted lemon butter from the bottom of the pot. Drizzle with lemon juice and serve.

Nutrition: Calories: 202 Fat: 13.4g Carbs: 1.3g Protein: 20.3g

Salmon with Green Beans

Preparation time: 10 minutes

Cooking time: 3 hours

Servings: 4

Ingredients:

- Salmon fillets – 4, skin on
- Garlic – 4 cloves, crushed
- Broccoli – ½ head, cut into florets
- Frozen green beans – 2 cups
- Olive oil – 3 tbsp., divided
- Salt and pepper to taste
- Water – ¼ cup

Directions:

1. Add the olive oil into the Crock-Pot.
2. Season the salmon with salt and pepper and place into the pot (skin-side down). Add the water.
3. Place garlic, beans, and broccoli on top of the salmon. Season with salt and pepper.
4. Drizzle some more oil over the veggies and fish.
5. Cover with the lid and cook on high for 3 hours.
6. Serve.

Nutrition: Calories: 278 Fat: 17.8g Carbs: 8.1g Protein: 24.5g

Coconut Fish Curry

Preparation time: 10 minutes

Cooking time: 4 hours

Servings: 4

Ingredients:

- Large white fish fillets – 4, cut into chunks
- Garlic cloves – 4, crushed
- Small onion – 1, finely chopped
- Ground turmeric – 1 tsp.
- Yellow curry paste – 2 tbsp.
- Fish stock – 2 cups
- Full-fat coconut milk – 2 cans
- Lime – 1
- Fresh coriander as needed, roughly chopped
- Olive oil – 2 tbsp.
- Salt and pepper to taste

Directions:

1. Add olive oil into the Crock-Pot.
2. Add the coconut milk, stock, fish, curry paste, turmeric, onion, garlic, salt, and pepper to the pot. Stir to combine.
3. Cover with the lid and cook on high for 4 hours.
4. Drizzle with lime juice and fresh coriander and serve.

Nutrition: Calories: 562 Fat: 49.9g Carbs: 13g Protein: 20.6g

Coconut Lime Mussels

Preparation time: 10 minutes

Cooking time: 2 ½ hours

Servings: 4

Ingredients:

- Fresh mussels – 16
- Garlic – 4 cloves
- Full-fat coconut milk – 1 ½ cups
- Red chili – ½, finely chopped
- Lime – 1, juiced
- Fish stock – ½ cup
- A handful of fresh coriander
- Olive oil – 2 tbsp.
- Salt and pepper to taste

Directions:

1. Add olive oil into the Crock-Pot.
2. Add the coconut milk, garlic, chili, fish stock, salt, pepper, and juice of one lime to the pot. Stir to mix.
3. Cover with the lid and cook on high for 2 hours.
4. Remove the lid, place mussels into the liquid, and cover with the lid.
5. Cook until mussels open, about 20 minutes.
6. Serve the mussels with pot sauce. Garnish with fresh coriander.

Nutrition: Calories: 342 Fat: 30.2g Carbs: 11.3g Protein: 10.9g

Calamari, Prawn, and Shrimp Pasta Sauce

Preparation time: 10 minutes

Cooking time: 3 hours

Servings: 4

Ingredients:

- Calamari – 1 cup
- Prawns – 1 cup
- Shrimp – 1 cup
- Garlic – 6 cloves, crushed
- Tomatoes – 4, chopped
- Dried mixed herbs – 1 tsp.
- Balsamic vinegar - 1 tbsp.
- Olive oil – 2 tbsp.
- Salt and pepper to taste
- Water – ½ cup

Directions:

1. Add oil into the Crock-Pot.
2. Add the tomatoes, garlic, shrimp, prawns, calamari, mixed herbs, balsamic vinegar, water, salt, and pepper. Stir to mix.
3. Cover with the lid and cook on high for 3 hours.
4. Serve with zucchini noodles or veggies.

Nutrition: Calories: 372 Fat: 14.6g Carbs: 8.5g Protein: 55.1g

Sesame Prawns

Preparation time: 10 minutes

Cooking time: 2 hours

Servings: 4

Ingredients:

- Large prawns – 3 cups
- Garlic – 4 cloves, crushed
- Sesame oil – 1 tbsp.
- Toasted sesame seeds – 2 tbsp.
- Red chili – ½, finely chopped
- Fish stock – ½ cup
- Salt and pepper to taste
- Chopped herbs for serving

Directions:

1. Drizzle the sesame oil into the Crock-Pot.
2. Add the garlic, prawns, sesame seeds, chili, and fish stock to the pot. Mix to coat.
3. Cover with the lid and cook on high for 2 hours.
4. Serve hot with fresh herbs and cauliflower rice.

Nutrition: Calories: 236 Fat: 7.7g Carbs: 4.3g Protein: 37.4g

Thyme Beef

Preparation time: 15 minutes

Cooking time: 5 hours

Servings: 2

Ingredients

- oz. beef sirloin, chopped
- 1 tablespoon dried thyme
- 1 tablespoon olive oil
- ½ cup of water
- 1 teaspoon salt

Directions

1. Preheat the skillet well.
2. Then mix beef with dried thyme and olive oil.
3. Put the meat in the hot skillet and roast for 2 minutes per side on high heat.
4. Then transfer the meat to the slow cooker.
5. Add salt and water.
6. Cook the meal on High for 5 hours.

Nutrition : 274 calories, 34.5g Protein, 0.9g carbohydrates, 14.2g fat, 0.5g fiber 101mg cholesterol, 1240mg sodium, 469 mg potassium

Hot Beef

Preparation time: 15 minutes

Cooking time: 8 hours

Servings: 4

Ingredients

- 1-pound beef sirloin, chopped
- 2 tablespoons hot sauce
- 1 tablespoon olive oil
- ½ cup of water

Directions

1. In the shallow bowl, mix hot sauce with olive oil.
2. Then mix beef sirloin with hot sauce mixture and leave for 10 minutes to marinate.
3. Put the marinated beef in the slow cooker.
4. Add water and close the lid.
5. Cook the meal on Low for 8 hours.

Nutrition : 241 calories, 34.4g Protein, 0.1g carbohydrates, 10.6g fat, 0g fiber, 101mg cholesterol, 266mg sodium, 467 mg potassium.

Beef Chops with Sprouts

Preparation time: 10 minutes

Cooking time: 7 hours

Servings: 5

Ingredients

- 1-pound beef loin
- ½ cup bean sprouts
- 1 cup of water
- 1 tablespoon tomato paste
- 1 teaspoon chili powder
- 1 teaspoon salt

Directions

1. Cut the beef loin into 5 beef chops and sprinkle the beef chops with chili powder and salt.
2. Then place them in the slow cooker.
3. Add water and tomato paste. Cook the meat on low for 7 hours.
4. Then transfer the cooked beef chops onto the plates, sprinkle with tomato gravy from the slow cooker, and top with bean sprouts.

Nutrition : 175 calories, 2 5.2g Protein, 1.6g carbohydrates, 7.8g fat, 0.3g fiber, 64mg cholesterol, 526mg sodium, 386 mg potassium.

Beef Ragout with Beans

Preparation time: 10 minutes

Cooking time: 5 hours

Servings: 5

Ingredients

- 1 tablespoon tomato paste
- 1 cup mug beans, canned
- 1 carrot, grated
- 1-pound beef stew meat, chopped
- 1 teaspoon ground black pepper
- 2 cups of water

Directions

1. Pour water into the slow cooker.
2. Add meat, ground black pepper, and carrot.
3. Cook the mixture on High for 4 hours.
4. Then add tomato paste and mug beans. Stir the meal and cook it on high for 1 hour more.

Nutrition : 321 calories, 37.7g Protein, 28g carbohydrates, 6.2g fat, 7.3g fiber, 81mg cholesterol, 81 mg sodium, 959 mg potassium.

Braised Beef

Preparation time: 8 minutes

Cooking time: 9 hours

Servings: 2

Ingredients

- oz. beef tenderloin, chopped
- 1 garlic clove, peeled
- 1 teaspoon peppercorn
- 1 teaspoon salt
- 1 tablespoon dried basil
- 2 cups of water

Directions

1. Put all **I**ngredients : from the list above in the slow cooker.
2. Gently stir the mixture and close the lid.
3. Cook the beef on low for 9 hours.

Nutrition : 239 calories, 33.1g Protein, 1.2g carbohydrates, 10.4g fat, 0.3g fiber, 104mg cholesterol, 1238mg sodium, 431 mg potassium.

Coconut Beef

Preparation time: 10 minutes

Cooking time: 8 hours

Servings: 5

Ingredients

- 1 cup baby spinach, chopped
- 1 cup of coconut milk
- 1-pound beef tenderloin, chopped
- 1 teaspoon avocado oil
- 1 teaspoon dried rosemary
- 1 teaspoon garlic powder

Directions

1. Roast meat in the avocado oil for 1 minute per side on high heat.
2. Then transfer the meat in the slow cooker.
3. Add garlic powder, dried rosemary, coconut milk, and baby spinach.
4. Close the lid and cook the meal on Low for 8 hours.

Nutrition : 303 calories, 27.6g Protein, 3.5g carbohydrates, 19.9g fat, 1.4g fiber, 83mg cholesterol, 66mg sodium, 495 mg potassium.

Beef Roast

Preparation time: 10 minutes

Cooking time: 6 hours

Servings: 5

Ingredients

- 1-pound beef chuck roast
- 1 tablespoon ketchup
- 1 tablespoon mayonnaise
- 1 teaspoon chili powder
- 1 teaspoon olive oil
- 1 teaspoon lemon juice
- ½ cup of water

Directions

1. In the bowl, mix ketchup, mayonnaise, chili powder, olive oil, and lemon juice.
2. Then sprinkle the beef chuck roast with ketchup mixture.
3. Pour the water into the slow cooker.
4. Add beef chuck roast and close the lid.
5. Cook the meat on High for 6 hours.

Nutrition : 354 calories, 23.9g, Protein, 1.8g carbohydrates, 27.3g fat, 0.2g fiber, 94mg cholesterol, 119mg sodium, 230 mg potassium.

Lunch Beef

Preparation time: 10 minutes

Cooking time: 8 hours

Servings: 2

Ingredients

- ½ white onion, sliced
- 1 teaspoon brown sugar
- 1 teaspoon chili powder
- 1 teaspoon hot sauce
- ½ cup okra, chopped
- 1 cup of water
- oz. beef loin, chopped

Directions

1. Mix the beef loin with hot sauce, chili powder, and brown sugar.
2. Transfer the meat to the slow cooker.
3. Add water, okra, and onion.
4. Cook the meal on Low for 8 hours.

Nutrition : 179 calories, 19.3g Protein, 7.8g carbohydrates, 7.4g fat, 1.8g fiber, 53mg cholesterol, 520mg sodium, 146 mg potassium.

Braised Beef Strips

Preparation time: 10 minutes

Cooking time: 5 hours

Servings: 4

Ingredients

- ½ cup mushroom, sliced
- 1 onion, sliced
- 1 cup of water
- 1 tablespoon coconut oil
- 1 teaspoon salt
- 1 teaspoon white pepper
- oz. beef loin, cut into strips

Directions

1. Melt the coconut oil in the skillet.
2. Add mushrooms and roast them for 5 minutes on medium heat.
3. Then transfer the mushrooms to the slow cooker.
4. Add all remaining **Ingredients:** and close the lid.
5. Cook the meal on High for 5 hours

Nutrition : 173 calories, 19.6g Protein, 3.2g carbohydrates, 9.4g fat, 0.8g fiber, 50mg cholesterol, 624mg sodium, 316 mg potassium.

Mexican Lamb Fillet

Preparation Time: 5 Minutes

Cooking Time: 8 Hours

Servings: 4

Ingredients:

- 1 chili pepper, deseeded and chopped
- 1 jalapeno pepper, deseeded and chopped
- 1 cup sweet corn
- 1 cup chicken stock
- 14 oz lamb fillet
- 1 tsp salt
- 1 tsp ground black pepper
- 1 tbsp ground paprika
- 1 tsp grated ginger
- 1 cup tomato juice
- 1 tbsp white sugar

Directions:

1. Add the peppers, ginger, and ground paprika to the blender jug.
2. Blend this peppers mixture for 30 seconds until smooth.
3. Place the lamb fillet to the insert of the Slow cooker.
4. Add pepper mixture, tomato juice, white sugar, black pepper, and salt to the lamb.
5. Lastly, add sweet corn and chicken stock.

6. Put the cooker's lid on and set the cooking time to 8 hours on Low settings.
7. Shred the cooked lamb and return the cooker.
8. Mix well and serve warm.

Nutrition: Calories: 348, Total Fat: 18.3g, Fiber: 3g, Total Carbs: 19.26g, Protein: 28g

Beef Mac & Cheese

Preparation Time: 5 Minutes

Cooking Time: 4 Hours and 30 Minutes

Servings: 4

Ingredients:

- ½ cup macaroni, cooked
- 10 oz ground beef
- ½ cup marinara sauce
- 1 cup Mozzarella, shredded
- ½ cup of water

Directions:

1. Mix the ground beef with marinara sauce and water and transfer in the Slow cooker.
2. Cook it on High for 4 hours.
3. After this, add macaroni and Mozzarella.
4. Carefully mix the meal and cook it for 30 minutes more on high.

Nutrition: 25.4g Protein, 12.4g Carbohydrates, 1.2g Fat, 68g Fiber, 63mg Cholesterol, 219mg Sodium, 408 mg Potassium.

Beef with Scallions Bowl

Preparation Time: 5 Minutes

Cooking Time: 5 Hours

Servings: 4

Ingredients:

- 1 teaspoon chili powder
- 2 oz scallions, chopped
- 1-pound beef stew meat, cubed
- 1 cup corn kernels, frozen
- 1 cup of water
- 2 tablespoons tomato paste
- 1 teaspoon minced garlic

Directions:

1. Mix water with tomato paste and pour the liquid into the Slow cooker.
2. Add chili powder, beef, corn kernels, and minced garlic.
3. Close the lid and cook the meal on high for 5 hours.
4. When the meal is cooked, transfer the mixture to the bowls and top with scallions.

Nutrition: 36.4g Protein, 10.4g Carbohydrates, 7.7g Fat, 2g Fiber, 101mg Cholesterol, 99mg Sodium, 697 mg Potassium.

Easy Balsamic Beef

Preparation Time: 5 Minutes

Cooking Time: 9 Hours

Servings: 4

Ingredients:

- 1-pound beef stew meat, cubed
- 1 teaspoon cayenne pepper
- 4 tablespoons balsamic vinegar
- ½ cup of water
- 2 tablespoons butter

Directions:

1. Toss the butter in the skillet and melt it.
2. Then add meat and roast it for minutes per side on medium heat.
3. Transfer the meat with butter in the Slow cooker.
4. Add balsamic vinegar, cayenne pepper, and water.
5. Close the lid and cook the meal on Low for 9 hours.

Nutrition: 34.5g Protein, 0.4g Carbohydrates, 12.9g Fat, 0.1g Fiber, 117mg Cholesterol, 117mg Sodium, 479 mg Potassium.

Simple Pork Chop Casserole

Preparation Time: 5 Minutes

Cooking Time: 10 Hours

Servings: 4

Ingredients:

- 4 pork chops, bones removed and cut into bite-sized pieces
- 3 tablespoons minced onion
- ½ cup of water
- Salt and pepper to taste
- 1 cup heavy cream

Directions:

1. Place the pork chop slices, onions, and water in the slow cooker.
2. Season with salt and pepper to taste.
3. Close the lid and cook on low for 10 hours or on high for 8 hours.
4. Halfway through the cooking time, pour in the heavy cream.

Nutrition: Calories per serving: 515; Carbohydrates: 2.5g; Protein: 39.2g; Fat: 34.3g; Sugar: 0g; Sodium: 613mg; Fiber: 0.9 g

Balsamic Lamb Chops

Preparation Time: 5 Minutes

Cooking Time: 6 Hours

Servings: 2

Ingredients:

- 1-pound lamb chops
- 2 tablespoons balsamic vinegar
- 1 tablespoon chives, chopped
- 1 tablespoon olive oil
- 4 garlic cloves, minced
- ½ cup beef stock
- A pinch of salt and black pepper

Directions:

1. In your Slow cooker, mix the lamb chops with the vinegar and the other ingredients, toss, put the lid on and cook on Low for 6 hours.
2. Divide everything between plates and serve.

Nutrition: Calories 292, Fat 12, Fiber 3, Carbs 7, Protein 16

Lamb and Cabbage

Preparation Time: 5 Minutes

Cooking Time: 5 Hours

Servings: 2

Ingredients:

- 2 pounds lamb stew meat, cubed
- 1 cup red cabbage, shredded
- 1 cup beef stock
- 1 teaspoon avocado oil
- 1 teaspoon sweet paprika
- 2 tablespoons tomato paste
- A pinch of salt and black pepper
- 1 tablespoon cilantro, chopped

Directions:

1. In your Slow cooker, mix the lamb with the cabbage, stock, and the other ingredients, toss, put the lid on and cook on High for 5 hours.
2. Divide everything between plates and serve.

Nutrition: Calories 254, Fat 12, Fiber 3, Carbs 6, Protein 16

Squash Noodles

Preparation time: 15 minutes

Cooking time: 4 hours

Servings: 4

Ingredients:

- 1-pound butternut squash, seeded, halved
- 1 tablespoon vegan butter
- 1 teaspoon salt
- ½ teaspoon garlic powder
- cups of water

Directions

1   Pour water in the slow cooker.

2   Add butternut squash and close the lid.

3   Cook the vegetable on high for 4 hours.

4   Then drain water and shred the squash flesh with the fork's help and transfer in the bowl.

5   Add garlic powder, salt, and butter. Mix the squash noodles.

Nutrition: 78 calories, 1.2g Protein, 13.5g carbohydrates, 3g fat, 2.3g fiber, 8mg cholesterol, 612mg sodium, 406mg potassium

Thyme Tomatoes

Preparation time: 10 minutes

Cooking time: 5 hours

Servings: 4

Ingredients:

- 1-pound tomatoes, sliced
- 1 tablespoon dried thyme
- 1 teaspoon salt
- tablespoons olive oil
- 1 tablespoon apple cider vinegar
- ½ cup of water

Directions

1   Place ingredients in the slow cooker and close the lid.

2   Cook the tomatoes on Low for 5 hours.

Nutrition: 83 calories, 1.1g Protein, 4.9g carbohydrates, 7.3g fat, 1.6g fiber, 0mg cholesterol, 588mg sodium, 277mg potassium

Quinoa Dolma

Preparation time: 15 minutes

Cooking time: 3 hours

Servings: 6

Ingredients:

- sweet peppers, seeded
- 1 cup quinoa, cooked
- ½ cup corn kernels, cooked
- 1 teaspoon chili flakes
- 1 cup of water
- ½ cup tomato juice

Directions

1   Mix quinoa with corn kernels, and chili flakes.

2   Fill the sweet peppers with quinoa mixture and put in the slow cooker.

3   Add water and tomato juice.

4   Close the lid and cook the peppers on High for 3 hours.

Nutrition: 171 calories, 6.6g Protein, 33.7g carbohydrates, 2.3g fat, 4.8g fiber, 0mg cholesterol, 29mg sodium, 641mg potassium

Creamy Puree

Preparation time: 10 minutes

Cooking time: 4 hours

Servings: 4

Ingredients:

- cups potatoes, chopped
- cups of water
- 1 tablespoon vegan butter
- ¼ cup cream
- 1 teaspoon salt

Directions

1   Pour water in the slow cooker.

2   Add potatoes and salt.

3   Cook the vegetables on high for 4 hours.

4   Then drain water, add butter, and cream.

5   Mash the potatoes until smooth.

Nutrition: 87 calories, 1.4g Protein, 12.3g carbohydrates, 3.8g fat, 1.8g fiber, 10mg cholesterol, 617mg sodium, 314mg potassium

Cauliflower Hash

Preparation time: 10 minutes

Cooking time: 2.5 hours

Servings: 4

Ingredients:

- cups cauliflower, roughly chopped
- ½ cup potato, chopped
- oz. Provolone, grated
- tablespoons chives, chopped
- 1 cup milk
- ½ cup of water
- 1 teaspoon chili powder

Directions

1   Pour water and milk in the slow cooker.

2   Add cauliflower, potato, chives, and chili powder.

3   Close the lid and cook the mixture on high for 2 hours.

4   Then sprinkle the hash with provolone cheese and cook the meal on High for 30 minutes.

Nutrition: 134 calories, 9.3g Protein, 9.5g carbohydrates, 7.1g fat, 2.4g fiber, 20mg cholesterol, 246mg sodium, 348mg potassium

Brussels Sprouts

Preparation time: 10 minutes

Cooking time: 2.5 hours

Servings: 4

Ingredients:

- 1-pound Brussels sprouts
- oz. tofu, chopped, cooked
- 1 teaspoon cayenne pepper
- cups of water
- 1 tablespoon vegan butter

Directions

1   Pour water in the slow cooker.

2   Add Brussels sprouts and cayenne pepper.

3   Cook the vegetables on high for 2.5 hours.

4   Then drain water and mix Brussels sprouts with butter and tofu.

5   Shake the vegetables gently.

Nutrition: 153 calories, 9.2g Protein, 10.8g carbohydrates, 9.3g fat, 4.4g fiber, 23mg cholesterol, 380mg sodium, 532mg potassium

Sautéed Garlic

Preparation time: 10 minutes

Cooking time: 6 hours

Servings: 4

Ingredients:

- oz. garlic cloves, peeled
- tablespoons lemon juice
- 1 teaspoon ground black pepper
- 1 cup of water
- 1 tablespoon vegan butter
- 1 bay leaf

Directions

1   Put all ingredients in the slow cooker.

2   Close the lid and cook the garlic on Low for 6 hours.

Nutrition: 135 calories, 4.7g Protein, 24.1g carbohydrates, 3.3g fat, 1.7g fiber, 8mg cholesterol, 36mg sodium, 303mg potassium

Cheesy Corn

Preparation time: 5 minutes

Cooking time: 5 hours

Servings: 5

Ingredients:

- cups corn kernels
- ½ cup Cheddar cheese, shredded
- 1 tablespoon vegan butter
- 1 teaspoon ground black pepper
- 1 teaspoon salt
- cups of water

Directions

1   Mix corn kernels with ground black pepper, butter, salt, and cheese.

2   Transfer the mixture in the slow cooker and add water.

3   Close the lid and cook the meal on Low for 5 hours.

Nutrition: 173 calories, 6.9g Protein, 23.6g carbohydrates, 7.5g fat, 3.5g fiber, 18mg cholesterol, 573mg sodium, 351mg potassium

Shredded Cabbage Sauté

Preparation time: 10 minutes

Cooking time: 6 hours

Servings: 4

Ingredients:

- cups white cabbage, shredded
- 1 cup tomato juice
- 1 teaspoon salt
- 1 teaspoon sugar
- 1 teaspoon dried oregano
- tablespoons olive oil
- 1 cup of water

Directions

1   Put all ingredients in the slow cooker.

2   Carefully mix all ingredients with the help of the spoon and close the lid.

3   Cook the cabbage sauté for 6 hours on Low.

Nutrition: 118 calories, 1.2g Protein, 6.9g carbohydrates, 10.6g fat, 1.7g fiber, 0mg cholesterol, 756mg sodium, 235mg potassium

Ranch Broccoli

Preparation time: 10 minutes

Cooking time: 1.5 hours

Servings: 3

Ingredients:

- cups broccoli
- 1 teaspoon chili flakes
- tablespoons ranch dressing
- cups of water

Directions

1   Put the broccoli in the slow cooker.

2   Add water and close the lid.

3   Cook the broccoli on high for 1.5 hours.

4   Then drain water and transfer the broccoli in the bowl.

5   Sprinkle it with chili flakes and ranch dressing. Shake the meal gently.

Nutrition: 34 calories, 2.7g Protein, 6.6g carbohydrates, 0.3g fat, 2.4g fiber, 0mg cholesterol, 91mg sodium, 291 mg potassium.

Sautéed Spinach

Preparation time: 10 minutes

Cooking time: 1 hours

Servings: 3

Ingredients:

- cups spinach
- 1 tablespoon vegan butter, softened
- cups of water
- oz Parmesan, grated
- 1 teaspoon pine nuts, crushed

Directions

1   Slice the spinach and put it in the slow cooker.

2   Add water and close the lid.

3   Cook the spinach on High for 1 hour.

4   Then drain water and put the cooked spinach in the bowl.

5   Add pine nuts, Parmesan, and butter.

6   Carefully mix the spinach.

Nutrition: 108 calories, 7.1g Protein, 1.9g carbohydrates, 8.7g fat, 0.7g fiber, 24mg cholesterol, 231mg sodium, 176 mg potassium.

Cheddar Mushrooms

Preparation time: 10 minutes

Cooking time: 6 hours

Servings: 4

Ingredients:

- cups cremini mushrooms, sliced
- 1 teaspoon dried oregano
- 1 teaspoon ground black pepper
- ½ teaspoon salt
- 1 cup Cheddar cheese, shredded
- 1 cup heavy cream
- 1 cup of water

Directions

1   Pour water and heavy cream in the slow cooker.

2   Add salt, ground black pepper, and dried oregano.

3   Then add sliced mushrooms, and Cheddar cheese.

4   Cook the meal on Low for 6 hours.

5   When the mushrooms are cooked, gently stir them
     and transfer in the serving plates.

Nutrition: 239 calories, 9.6g Protein, 4.8g carbohydrates,
20.6g fat, 0.7g fiber, 71mg cholesterol, 484mg sodium, 386
mg potassium.

Fragrant Appetizer Peppers

Preparation time: 15 minutes

Cooking time: 1.5 hours

Servings: 2

Ingredients:

- sweet peppers, seeded
- ¼ cup apple cider vinegar
- 1 red onion, sliced
- 1 teaspoon peppercorns
- ½ teaspoon sugar
- ¼ cup of water
- 1 tablespoon olive oil

Directions

1   Slice the sweet peppers roughly and put in the slow cooker.

2   Cook the peppers on high for 1.5 hours.

3   Then cool the peppers well and store them in the fridge for up to 6 days.

Nutrition: 171 calories, 3.1g Protein, 25.1g carbohydrates, 7.7g fat, 4.7g fiber, 0mg cholesterol, 11mg sodium, 564 mg potassium.

Paprika Baby Carrot

Preparation time: 10 minutes

Cooking time: 2.5 hours

Servings: 2

Ingredients:

- 1 tablespoon ground paprika
- cups baby carrot
- 1 teaspoon cumin seeds
- 1 cup of water
- 1 teaspoon vegan butter

Directions

1   Pour water in the slow cooker.

2   Add baby carrot, cumin seeds, and ground paprika.

3   Close the lid and cook the carrot on High for 2.5 hours.

4   Then drain water, add butter, and shake the vegetables.

Nutrition: 60 calories, 1.6g Protein, 8.6g carbohydrates, 2.7g fat, 4.2g fiber, 5mg cholesterol, 64mg sodium, 220 mg potassium.

Butter Asparagus

Preparation time: 15 minutes

Cooking time: 5 hours

Servings: 4

Ingredients:

- 1-pound asparagus
- tablespoons vegan butter
- 1 teaspoon ground black pepper
- 1 cup vegetable stock

Directions

1   Pour the vegetable stock in the slow cooker.

2   Chop the asparagus roughly and add in the slow cooker.

3   Close the lid and cook the asparagus for 5 hours on Low.

4   Then drain water and transfer the asparagus in the bowl.

5   Sprinkle it with ground black pepper and butter.

Nutrition; 77 calories, 2.8g Protein, 4.9g carbohydrates, 6.1g fat, 2.5g fiber, 15 mg cholesterol, 234 mg sodium, 241 mg potassium.

Jalapeno Corn

Preparation time: 10 minutes

Cooking time: 5 hours

Servings: 4

Ingredients:

- 1 cup heavy cream
- ½ cup Monterey Jack cheese, shredded
- 1-pound corn kernels
- jalapenos, minced
- 1 teaspoon vegan butter
- 1 tablespoon dried dill

Directions

1. Pour heavy cream in the slow cooker.
2. Add Monterey Jack cheese, corn kernels, minced jalapeno, butter, and dried dill.
3. Cook the corn on Low for 5 hours.

Nutrition: 203 calories, 5.6g Protein, 9.3g carbohydrates, 16.9g fat, 1.5g fiber, 56mg cholesterol, 101 mg sodium, 187 mg potassium.

Cauliflower Mash

Preparation time: 15 minutes

Cooking time: 3 hours

Servings: 4 people

Ingredients:

- 1 head cauliflower, cut into bite-sized pieces
- 5 garlic cloves, smashed
- 4 cup vegetable broth
- 1/3 cup Greek yogurt
- 3 tbsp. butter, cut into cubes
- 2 tbsp. fresh chives, chopped
- 1 tbsp. fresh parsley, chopped
- 1 tbsp. fresh rosemary, chopped
- 1 tsp. garlic powder
- Salt
- ground black pepper, to taste

Directions:

1. In a slow cooker, place the cauliflower, garlic, and broth and stir to combine. Cook, covered for about 2 to 3 hours on high.

2. Uncover the slow cooker and through a strainer, drain the cauliflower and garlic, reserving ½ cup of the broth. Transfer the cauliflower into a bowl, and with a potato masher, mash the cauliflower slightly.

3. Add the yogurt, butter, and desired amount of reserved broth and mash until smooth. Add the herbs, garlic powder, salt, and black pepper and stir to combine. Serve warm.

Nutrition: Calories: 105 Carbohydrates: 5.4g Protein: 5.3g Fat: 7g

Meat-Free Mushroom Stroganoff

Preparation time: 10 minutes

Cooking time: 5 hours

Servings: 3 people

Ingredients:

- 1¼ lb. fresh mushrooms, halved
- 1 onion, sliced thinly
- 3 garlic cloves, minced
- 2 tsp. smoked paprika
- 1 cup vegetable broth
- 1 tbsp. sour cream
- Salt
- ground black pepper
- 4 tbsp. fresh parsley, chopped

Directions:

1. In a slow cooker, place the mushrooms, onion, garlic, paprika, and broth and stir to combine. Set the slow cooker on high and cook, covered for about 4 hours.
2. Uncover the slow cooker and stir in the sour cream, salt, and black pepper. Serve with the garnishing of parsley.

Nutrition: Calories: 87 Carbohydrates: 12.2g Protein: 8.6g Fat: 2.1g

Veggies Ratatouille

Preparation time: 15 minutes

Cooking time: 6 hours

Servings: 4 people

Ingredients:

- 1 cup fresh basil
- 3 garlic cloves, minced
- 1/3 cup olive oil
- 2 tbsp. white wine vinegar
- 2 tbsp. fresh lemon juice
- 2 tbsp. tomato paste
- Salt, to taste
- 2 medium zucchinis, cut into small chunks
- 2 medium summer squash, cut into small chunks
- 1 small eggplant, cut into small chunks
- 1 large white onion, cut into small chunks
- 2 cup cherry tomatoes

Directions:

1. In a food processor, add the basil, garlic, oil, vinegar, lemon juice, tomato paste, salt, and pulse until smooth.

2. Put all the vegetables and top with the pureed mixture evenly in the bottom of a slow cooker. Cook, covered for about 5-6 hours on low. Serve hot.

Nutrition: Calories: 125 Carbohydrates: 11.5g Protein: 2.7g Fat: 8.9g

Colorful Veggie Combo

Preparation time: 15 minutes

Cooking time: 3 hours

Servings: 4 people

Ingredients:

- 1 tbsp. olive oil
- 1 lb. eggplant, peeled and cut into 1-inch cubes
- 1 small zucchini, chopped
- 1 small yellow squash, chopped
- 1 small orange bell pepper, seeded and chopped
- 1 small yellow bell pepper, seeded and chopped
- 1 large red onion, chopped
- 4 plum tomatoes, chopped
- 4 garlic cloves, minced
- 2 tsp. dried basil
- Salt
- ground black pepper, to taste
- 4 oz. feta cheese, crumbled

Directions:

1. In a slow cooker, place all the ingredients except for cheese and stir to combine. Cook, covered for about 3 hours on high. Serve hot with the topping of feta cheese.

Nutrition: Calories: 203 Carbohydrates: 23.6g Protein: 8.1g Fat: 190.3

Zucchini Balls

Preparation time: 20 minutes

Cooking time: 30 minutes

Servings: 4

Ingredients

- 1 cup zucchini, grated
- ½ cup almond flour
- ¼ cup Parmesan, grated
- 1 egg, whisked
- 1 tablespoon avocado oil
- ¾ cup of coconut milk
- ½ teaspoon salt

Directions:

1. In the mixing bowl zucchinis with flour and the other **Ingredients:** except the coconut milk and the oil and shape medium balls.
2. Preheat avocado oil in the skillet and add zucchini balls.
3. Roast them for 2 minutes from each side.
4. After this, transfer the zucchini balls in the slow cooker. Add coconut milk and close the lid.
5. Cook the meal for 30 minutes on High.

Nutrition : Calories 207, Fat 5.5, Fibre 1.8, Carbs, 4.5, Protein 3.6

Delightful Dal

Preparation Time: 15 Minutes

Cooking Time: 7 Hours

Servings: 4

Ingredients:

- 3 cups red lentils, rinsed
- 6 cups water
- 1 (28-ounce) can diced tomatoes, with juice
- 1 small yellow onion, diced
- 2½ teaspoons minced garlic (5 cloves)
- 1 (1-inch) piece fresh ginger, peeled and minced
- 1 tablespoon ground turmeric
- 2 teaspoons ground cumin
- 1½ teaspoons ground cardamom
- 1½ teaspoons whole mustard seeds
- 1 teaspoon fennel seeds
- 1 bay leaf
- 1 teaspoon salt
- ¼ teaspoon freshly ground black pepper

Directions:

1. Combine the lentils, water, diced tomatoes, onion, garlic, ginger, turmeric, cumin, cardamom, mustard seeds, fennel seeds, bay leaf, salt, and pepper in a slow cooker; mix well.

2. Cover and cook on low for 7 to 9 hours or on high for 4 to 6 hours.
3. Remove the bay leaf, and serve.

Nutrition: Calories: 585; Total fat: 4g; Protein: 40g; Sodium: 616mg; Fiber: 48g

Moroccan Chickpea Stew

Preparation Time: 15 Minutes

Cooking Time: 8 Hours

Servings: 4

Ingredients:

- 1 small butternut squash, peeled and chopped into bite-size pieces
- 3 cups Very Easy Vegetable Broth or store-bought
- 1 medium yellow onion, diced
- 1 bell pepper, diced
- 1 (15-ounce) can chickpeas, drained and rinsed
- 1 (14.5-ounce) can tomato sauce
- ¾ cup brown lentils, rinsed
- 1½ teaspoons minced garlic (3 cloves)
- 1½ teaspoons ground ginger
- 1½ teaspoons ground turmeric
- 1½ teaspoons ground cumin
- 1 teaspoon ground cinnamon
- ¾ teaspoon smoked paprika
- ½ teaspoon salt
- 1 (8-ounce) package fresh udon noodles
- Freshly ground black pepper

Directions:

1. Combine the butternut squash, vegetable broth, onion, bell pepper, chickpeas, tomato sauce, brown

lentils, garlic, ginger, turmeric, cumin, cinnamon, smoked paprika, and salt in a slow cooker. Mix well.

2. Cover and cook 6 to 8 hours on low or 3 to 4 hours on high. In the last 10 minutes of cooking, add the noodles.

3. Season with pepper, and serve.

Nutrition: Calories: 427; Total fat: 4g; Protein: 26g; Sodium: 1,423mg; Fiber: 24g

Tex-Mex Taco Filling

Preparation Time: 15 Minutes

Cooking Time: 8 Hours

Servings: 4

Ingredients:

- 2 cups Very Easy Vegetable Broth or store-bought
- 1 cup green lentils, rinsed
- ½ cup uncooked quinoa, rinsed
- ¼ cup finely diced yellow onion
- 1½ teaspoons minced garlic (3 cloves)
- 2 teaspoons ground cumin
- 1 teaspoon chili powder
- ½ teaspoon smoked paprika
- Pinch salt
- Freshly ground black pepper
- Tortillas or taco shells, for serving
- Optional toppings: Nacho Cheese, Guacamole, minced onions, sliced radishes, cilantro, or hot sauce

Directions:

1. Combine the vegetable broth, lentils, quinoa, onion, garlic, cumin, chili powder, and smoked paprika in a slow cooker. Mix well.
2. Cover and cook on low for 7 to 8 hours.
3. Season with salt and pepper.

4. Serve with tortillas or taco shells and your choice of toppings.

Nutrition: Calories: 283; Total fat: 3g; Protein: 14g; Sodium: 434mg; Fiber: 17g

Lightning Source UK Ltd.
Milton Keynes UK
UKHW022317290721
388013UK00002B/322